D1443745

TREES

Martin Gitlin

Rourke
Educational Media

rourkeeducationalmedia.com

★ ★ ★ ★ ★ ★ ★ ■ Introduction ■ ★ ★ ★ ★ ★ ★ ★

Some stand with majesty in size and strength. Others look small and pretty. They are the trees of America. And many have been honored by the states in which they grow.

Travelers view them with joy as they drive past gorgeous scenery. Visitors to forests and state parks marvel at them. They decorate lawns. They provide a lovely and clean look to city streets. They add to the charm of country settings. They display leaves that change into stunning colors.

But state trees do not merely serve as eye candy. They bear fruit or sap used to make maple or pine syrup. They produce wood needed for many products. They can be adorned for Christmas. They can even be climbed for fun.

They can be tiny or tall. Their trunks can be skinny or fat. Their branches can be short or long. Their leaves can be round or pointy. They can be green or red or brown or yellow. And they all give a sense of pride to residents of their states.

What makes these trees all special? You can learn about every one of them right here!

★★★★★★★★ Contents ★★★★★★★★

Southern Longleaf Pine

The favorite home of the rare red-cockaded woodpecker thrives in areas with long, hot summers. The wood from this tall pine was once used to build ships. It now goes into flooring.

Sap-to-Syrup Ratio

It takes about 40 gallons (151 liters) of sap extracted from the southern longleaf pine to make one gallon (3.79 liters) of syrup. But the sweet liquid you pour on pancakes is not all that comes from the pine. Its wood has also been turned into the lanes you bowl on at the bowling alley.

Average Height:	Lifespan:	Year Adopted:	Scientific Name:
98 –115 feet (29.87 – 35.05 meters)	300 years	1949	*Pinus palustris*

Sitka Spruce

A tolerance to salt spray allows the world's largest-growing spruce to thrive close to the seashore. Its high-grade lumber has been used to build airplanes.

Strumming with a Sitka

A luthier is an artist that creates stringed instruments. And luthiers prefer the Sitka spruce wood when crafting guitars. The wooden planks on which pirates forced enemies to walk before they plunged into the water? They too were made from Sitka wood. Arrghh!

Average Height:	Lifespan:	Year Adopted:	Scientific Name:
160 feet (48.77 meters)	700 years	1962	*Picea sitchensis*

Palo Verde

Green bark and droopy branches reaching the ground liven up the Arizona desert. A palo verde will often grow near a saguaro cactus, the state flower.

They All Hang Around

This tree is quite an attraction to the animals of Arizona. Among those that look for food and shelter around the palo verde are bighorn sheep, mule deer, and jackrabbits. Many birds seek food or nest in its many branches.

Average Height:	Lifespan:	Year Adopted:	Scientific Name:
20 feet (6.09 meters)	100 – 400 years	1954	Cercidium

Pine

The oddly named loblolly pine is often considered the state tree. But the most common in Arkansas is the shortleaf pine. These varieties of pine cover more than five million acres (2,023,428 hectares) of forest land in this state.

Hello, Morris Pine!

The most famous tree in southeastern Arkansas is the Morris Pine. The ancient loblolly has served to greet visitors for more than 50 years. It is estimated to have lived more than 300 years on the grounds of a forest near the town of Hamburg.

Average Height:	Lifespan:	Year Adopted:	Scientific Name:
98 – 115 feet (29.87 – 35.05 meters)	200 years	1939	*pinus* family

7

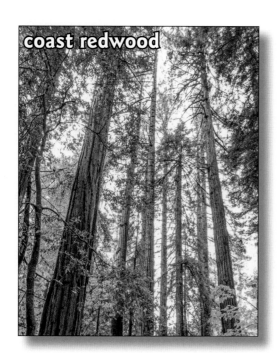

coast redwood

giant Sequoia

Coast Redwood; Giant Sequoia

California adopted two species of redwood as their state trees, the coast redwood and the giant Sequoia. The coast redwoods thrive along the rainy, foggy coast. These tallest of trees reach heights of more than 350 feet (107 m). Redwoods can achieve a diameter of 24 feet (7 m). The other state tree honors Indian chief Sequoya. He invented the Cherokee alphabet.

Now That's Old!

The earliest redwood trees showed up on Earth soon after the dinosaurs—and before flowers, birds, and people. It is estimated that redwoods have populated the planet for about 240 million years. Modern humans have been around for 200 thousand years.

Average Height:	Lifespan:	Year Adopted:	Scientific Name:
coast redwood 350 feet+ (107 meters)	up to 2,000 years	1937	Sequoia sempervirens
giant Sequoia up to 370 feet (112.78 meters)	2,500-3,500 years	1937	Sequoia-dendron giganteum

Blue Spruce

The sharp needles and stiff branches of the blue spruce make decorating one for Christmas quite a task! A campaign to teach Colorado kids about local trees led to its adoption.

Big Winds? No Problem

The blue spruce withstands strong winds better than most spruces. That is because of its wide-spreading branches and fairly deep roots. The leaves of this tree do not change color. The unique silvery bluish green remains all year long.

Average Height:	Lifespan:	Year Adopted:	Scientific Name:
50 –70 feet (15.24 – 21.34 meters)	200 years	1939	*Picea pungens*

White Oak

One white oak gained fame in 1687. That is when a document demanding colony rights was hidden in its hollow from British agents. The event inspired Connecticut to adopt the white oak as its state tree.

Sadly Fading Away

The white oak is legendary in Connecticut. But there are certainly a lot fewer of them than there were in Colonial times. Many have died due to the clearing of forests, grazing of deer, and large fires.

Average Height:	Lifespan:	Year Adopted:	Scientific Name:
50 – 80 feet (15.24 – 24.38 meters)	300 years	1947	Quercus alba

American Holly

Prickly green leaves and red berries make this tree special. The American Holly is dwarfed by other trees in the Delaware forests. Its wood makes tool handles and even piano keys.

A Winter Wonder

Evergreen holly trees are of great interest in the winter. That is when they display bright foliage while other trees become bare. That is also when the bright holly berries are displayed. They are inedible to humans, but they provide food for birds and other wildlife.

Average Height:	Lifespan:	Year Adopted:	Scientific Name:
40 –50 feet (12.19 – 15.24 meters)	100 years	1939	Ilex opaca

Cabbage, or Sabal, Palmetto

No state is better known for its palm trees than sunny Florida. This state tree features unbranched trunks and five-foot (152.4 centimeter) leaves. An image of the cabbage palm adorns the state flag.

Not Just a Pretty Tree

Many products come from various palm species. The most obvious is the coconut, which grows wild just underneath the branches. But palms also provide dates and other fruit. The Pindo palm produces an orange-yellow fruit used to make jelly. Palm oil used for cooking comes from the fruit of the oil palm tree.

Average Height:	Lifespan:	Year Adopted:	Scientific Name:
40 – 50 feet (12.19 –15.24 meters)	200 – 300 years	1953	Sabal palmetto

Southern Live Oak

This massive tree featuring wood once used for ship-building often grows more wide than tall. Its short trunk and long branches sometimes result in Spanish moss dangling to the ground.

Out with the Old, In with the New

Why is this tree called a live oak? Because it keeps its leaves year-round. That is not true with other oaks, which become barren in the winter. The live oak produces new leaves to replace the ones that fall off.

Average Height:	Lifespan:	Year Adopted:	Scientific Name:
50 feet (15.24 meters)	300 years	1937	*Quercus virginia*

Candlenut Tree

The candlenut, which yields oil for soap, is not native to Hawaii. It was transported by Polynesian settlers. But Hawaii switched its state tree from the coconut palm in 1959.

A Bit Odd, But True

The candlenut tree is also called a kukui. It is ironic for a tree to be used to make a product that burns down. But the candlenut received its name by early settlers in native lands who used its nuts to make candles.

Average Height:	Lifespan:	Year Adopted:	Scientific Name:
49 – 82 feet (14.94 – 24.99 meters)	220 years	1959	*Aleurites moluccana*

★ ★ ★ ★ ★ ★ ★ ★   ★ ★ ★ ★ ★ ★ ★ ★ ★

Western White Pine

This tall, upright tree used mostly for lumber features blue-green needles that grow in groups of five. The white pine once thrived in the Idaho panhandle and grew up to 200 feet (60.96 meters).

That Bad Blister Rust

The western white pine has widely died out for many reasons. The most destructive cause is a disease called white pine blister rust. It became an epidemic in Idaho by the 1940s. Rust resistant seedlings were planted, but the new trees populate only a small amount of the land they once occupied.

Average Height:	Lifespan:	Year Adopted:	Scientific Name:
98–164 feet (29.87 – 49.99 meters)	150 – 250 years	1935	*Pinus monticola*

White Oak

People and animals wanting to cool off in hot weather often seek out white oaks. Their widely spreading branches make them ideal shade trees. Their beautiful leaves turn red and purple in the fall.

All About Acorns

White oaks start to produce acorns when they are about 20 years old. The number of acorns a tree produces varies year to year. Those that fall to the ground serve as important food for many kinds of birds and other animals in Illinois.

Average Height:	Lifespan:	Year Adopted:	Scientific Name:
50–80 feet (15.24–24.38 meters)	300 years	1973	Quercus alba

Tulip Poplar

The tall-trunked poplar is sure popular in Indiana. Pretty green, yellow, and orange flowers grow near the top. The flowers often remain unseen until they fall to the ground.

(Indiana continued)

The Popular Poplar

The tulip poplar is the tallest hardwood tree in North America. It can reach up to 150 feet (45.7 meters), though some are just half that size. The trunk often grows at least 50 feet (15.24 meters) without a single branch.

Average Height:	Lifespan:	Year Adopted:	Scientific Name:
70 – 90 feet (21.34 – 27.43 meters)	300 years	1931	Liriodendron tulipifera

 # Iowa

Oak

Iowa has not adopted any species as its state tree. But its bur oak is quite common. Folks should avoid standing under them. Their huge acorns prove quite painful when they fall on one's head.

Why the Oak?

Iowa officials chose the oak not just for the number that populate the state. It was also selected for the shelter, food, and nesting it provides the many birds and other animals of Iowa. Deer, turkeys, raccoons, squirrels, chipmunks, and woodpeckers are just some of the creatures that eat the acorns produced by Iowa oaks.

Average Height:	Lifespan:	Year Adopted:	Scientific Name:
70 feet (21.34 meters)	150 – 300 years	1961	Quercus family

Eastern Cottonwood

Kansas sits squarely in the Midwest, but it has adopted the eastern cottonwood as its own. The stout, wide-branching tree thrives near rivers, streams, and swamps.

Mississippi?

The largest eastern cottonwood tree plantation in the world is in Mississippi. Yet Kansas and Nebraska are the only two states that have adopted it as their official tree. Its buds are used to make a salve that relieves arthritis pain.

Average Height:	Lifespan:	Year Adopted:	Scientific Name:
65 – 130 feet (19.81 – 39.62 meters)	70 – 100 years	1937	*Populus deltoides*

Tulip Poplar

Make up your mind, Bluegrass State! Kentucky deemed this its unofficial state tree in 1956. But it officially adopted the coffee tree in 1976. It then switched in 1994 to the tulip poplar. The tree had many uses for famous settlers such as Daniel Boone.

Taking its Sweet Time

There are no tulips on the young tulip poplar. One cannot expect a recently planted tulip poplar to look as pretty as those that have had time to grow. A typical tulip poplar does not bloom tulips from its branches until it is about 15 years old.

Average Height:	Lifespan:	Year Adopted:	Scientific Name:
70 – 90 feet (21.34 – 27.43 meters)	100 – 300 years	1994	*Liriodendron tulipifera*

Bald Cypress

Southern swamps house this unique tree with half-inch needles and a lifespan of up to 2,000 years. Logging of the bald cypress once fed the Louisiana economy.

Playground for Critters

The bald cypress swamps this tree grows in are home to plenty of animal activity. Frogs, toads, and salamanders use the areas as breeding grounds. Wood ducks nest in hollow trunks, while bald eagles make their homes in the treetops.

Average Height:	Lifespan:	Year Adopted:	Scientific Name:
100 – 130 feet (30.48 – 39.62 meters)	600 years	1963	*Taxodium distichum*

Maine

Eastern White Pine

The tallest tree in Eastern North America is part of history. The British tried to hog its timber to make ship masts for their navy. That fueled the rebellion among New England that led to the Revolutionary War.

Timberrrrrrr!

The light, strong wood produced by the eastern white pine has been used to make toys, boxes, and cabinets. But the tree is also critical to wildlife. Its seeds feed such animals as squirrels, deer, mice, and many songbirds that whistle happy tunes for human visitors.

Average Height:	Lifespan:	Year Adopted:	Scientific Name:
80 – 100 feet (24.38 – 30.48 meters)	200 years	1945	*Pinus strobus*

Maryland

White Oak

A 2002 thunderstorm toppled the 460-year-old Wye Oak of Maryland. But the famous tree lives on. The National Grove of State Trees features white oaks grown from Wye Oak acorns.

Worth the Wait

This tree requires about 50 years of growth to start making acorns. But then it begins producing about 10 thousand every year. American Indians ground those acorns into flour centuries ago. They shared their technique with European settlers.

Average Height:	Lifespan:	Year Adopted:	Scientific Name:
50 – 80 feet (15.24 – 24.38 meters)	300 years	1941	*Quercus alba*

Massachusetts

American Elm

Massachusetts adopted this tall-trunked tree with arching branches in the 1940s. That is when it began falling victim to Dutch elm disease. The American elm still brings beauty to parks and streets.

(Massachusetts continued)

Strange Leaves

The two sides of every American elm leaf are quite different. One side is green and smooth. The other is much more pale and soft. The leaves of the American elm also feature about 15 pairs of veins.

Average Height:	Lifespan:	Year Adopted:	Scientific Name:
45 – 60 feet (13.72 – 18.29 meters)	175 – 300 years	1941	*Ulmus americana*

★ ★ ★ ★ ★ ★ ★ ★ ★ **Michigan** ★ ★ ★ ★ ★ ★ ★ ★ ★

Eastern White Pine

Logging and firestorms destroyed the pine that once thrived in Michigan forests. Beech and maple trees have become far more common.

Merry Christmas!

You can sometimes find folks in Michigan picking out eastern white pines to place in their homes as Christmas trees. The trees are also often used to beautify areas outside of houses and office buildings.

Average Height:	Lifespan:	Year Adopted:	Scientific Name:
80 – 100 feet (24.38 – 30.48 meters)	200 years	1955	*Pinus strobus*

Red Pine

A tree named for its reddish bark grows in cold Northern Minnesota. The tallest red pine in America stands at 126 feet (38.4 meters). It hovers over the others in Itasca State Park.

Using a Tree to Make a Call?

Many telephone poles in Minnesota and nearby states are made of wood from this tree. Red pine timber has been used in a variety of other ways for centuries. Among them was to build log cabins.

Average Height:	Lifespan:	Year Adopted:	Scientific Name:
90 – 100 feet (27.43– 30.48 meters)	250 years	1953	Pinus resinosa

Magnolia

The sweet-smelling magnolia that serves as the state flower grows on this large evergreen. The tree features stiff, dark, shiny green leaves. Its wood is used to make furniture and baskets.

A World Tree

There are more than 200 magnolia species that differ in size, shape, and flower color. They are native to Southeast Asia and North America. But their beauty has motivated plantings all over the world.

Average Height:	Lifespan:	Year Adopted:	Scientific Name:
15 – 80 feet (4.58 – 24.38 meters)	80 – 120 years	1938	*Magnolia grandiflora*

Flowering Dogwood

There are many varieties of the flowering dogwood, which produce a variety of different colored blooms. Clusters of red berries form in the fall. That season also shows the striking beauty of bright red leaves.

The United States and Beyond

This tree does not just make its home in America. It can be found in southern areas of Canada and eastern Mexico. The flowering dogwood can be seen in the eastern United States as far south as Florida and as far north as Maine.

Average Height:	Lifespan:	Year Adopted:	Scientific Name:
20 – 30 feet (6.09 – 9.14 meters)	80 years	1955	Cornus florida

★★★★★★★★ Montana ★★★★★★★★★

Ponderosa Pine

School children in the state capital of Helena chose this tall, black-barked pine as the state tree. It serves as the primary lumber tree of Montana.

(Montana continued)

One Important Tree

The only timber species considered more useful in western North America is the Douglas fir. Wood from the ponderosa pine in forests of the northwest region of the United States have been used to build doors, windows, and a variety of furniture.

Average Height:	Lifespan:	Year Adopted:	Scientific Name:
100 – 150 feet (30.48 – 45.72 meters)	300 years	1949	*Pinus ponderosa*

Nebraska

Eastern Cottonwood

One of the few trees to thrive on the Great Plains can mature in 10 years. Its cottony seeds often fall off and blow about in the wind. A big tree produces large drifts of seed-cotton on the ground.

Scared Leaves?

The long, flat stems of eastern cottonwood leaves make them vulnerable to wind. They tend to shake even in the mildest breeze. That is why they are known as "trembling leaves." But the wood is hard enough to be used to build barns and houses.

Average Height:	Lifespan:	Year Adopted:	Scientific Name:
65 – 130 feet (19.81 – 39.62 meters)	70 – 100 years	1972	*Populus deltoides*

single leaf pinyon pine

bristlecone pine

Single Leaf Pinyon Pine; Bristlecone Pine

Nevada added the bristlecone pine as a second state tree in 1987. They thrive in cold, dry areas near mountain tops. Their slow growth results in dense wood and survival against insects and rot.

Older Than Methuselah!

A single bristlecone pine in the White Mountains of California still stood in 2016 at the age of 4,848 years old. It was nicknamed Methuselah after a long-living Biblical character. In 2013, it lost its billing as the oldest of its species. That's when older one was discovered in the Inyo National Forest, which spans California and Nevada. That one is more than 5,000 years old!

Average Height:	Lifespan:	Year Adopted:	Scientific Name:
Single-leaf pinyon 33 – 66 feet (10.06 – 20.12 meters)	350 – 450 years	1959	*Pinus monphylla*
bristlecone pine 30 – 60 feet (9.14 – 18.8 meters)	1,000 years	1987	*Pinus longaeva*

Paper Birch

Those who get food stuck in their teeth can thank this cold-weather tree for removing it. Its wood is used to make toothpicks. Its white bark has been peeled in large strips to build canoes.

Keeping Hands from Getting Sticky

Those yummy ice cream bars and popsicles? They would be quite messy to eat if not for the light and strong wood of the paper birch. That is what is used to make the sticks attached to those treats.

Average Height:	Lifespan:	Year Adopted:	Scientific Name:
50 –70 feet (15.24 – 21.34 meters)	80 – 100 years	1947	*Betula papyrifera*

Northern Red Oak

Among the most colorful trees anywhere, the northern red oak boasts a vibrant red beauty in full bloom. It grows up to only 90 feet (27.43 meters) tall as its many branches spread out above its short base.

The Leaves That Do Not Leave

Trees are called "deciduous" if their leaves fall and they become barren in the winter. The northern red oak is not deciduous. Many of its leaves stay attached when fall turns into winter. That protects the trees from disease. It reduces the number of wounds caused when leaf stems detach from branches.

Average Height:	Lifespan:	Year Adopted:	Scientific Name:
65 – 90 feet (19.81 – 27.43 meters)	200 years	1950	*Quercus rubra*

Pinyon Pine

The pinyon tolerates desert conditions better than any American pine. It boasts thick, curved needles and grows edible seeds called pinyon nuts. They are usually roasted before eaten.

Nuts About Those Nuts

The jays and wild turkeys of New Mexico spend much time gobbling down pinyon nuts. But they are not alone. Among the other creatures that depend on the nuts as a food source are black bears, squirrels, mice, and chipmunks. Porcupines munch on the pinyon nuts as well, but prefer the bark.

Average Height:	Lifespan:	Year Adopted:	Scientific Name:
33 – 66 feet (10.06 – 20.12 meters)	350 – 450 years	1949	*Pinus edulis*

New York

Sugar Maple

This tree makes pancakes and waffles sweeter. Its sap is tapped and boiled down to form pure maple syrup. It also serves as eye candy with beautiful leaves that turn orange and red.

"Buy Your Maple Syrup Here!"

Written accounts of maple sugar production trace back to the early 1600s. That is when European explorers watched American Indians gathering sap. Maple syrup remains a popular item at roadside stands in New York and other northeastern states.

Average Height:	Lifespan:	Year Adopted:	Scientific Name:
30 – 35 feet (9.14 – 10.67 meters)	300 years	1956	Acer saccharum

North Carolina

Longleaf Pine

This rather fast-growing tree lives for up to 300 years. It produces lumber, rosin, and tar. But logging and other activities have wiped out nearly every longleaf pine forest in North Carolina.

(North Carolina continued)

The Sun-Loving Pine

The longleaf pine needs sun—lots of it. It prefers at least four hours of direct sunlight every day to grow at its best. Its height can increase more than two feet (.61 meters) per year if it receives the desired amount of sunlight.

Average Height:	Lifespan:	Year Adopted:	Scientific Name:
98 – 115 feet (29.87 – 35.05 meters)	300 years	1953	*Pinus palustris*

 # North Dakota

American Elm

The bark beetles spread Dutch elm disease in 1973. But the American elm remains plentiful in North Dakota. Two new varieties have shown a high resistance to the disease.

Brrrrrr ... Braving the Cold

This tree can survive very cold weather, which allows it to endure in the winter. It has been known to withstand temperatures as low as minus-44 degrees Fahrenheit (minus-6.6 degrees Celsius)!

Average Height:	Lifespan:	Year Adopted:	Scientific Name:
45 – 60 feet (13.72 – 1829 meters)	175 – 300 years	1947	*Ulmus americana*

Buckeye

The Buckeye produces buckeye nuts in the Buckeye State. The Ohio State University sports teams are called the Buckeyes. Buckeyes can only be eaten if removed from their shells and roasted. They look similar to chestnuts.

The Old Buckeye Jingle

The Buckeye State got its nickname during the campaign of ninth president William Henry Harrison. The Ohio native had log cabins of buckeye wood towed from town to town. Meanwhile, his supporters sang a jingle. It included the line, "Oh where, tell me where was the buckeye cabin made?" The tune spread images of buckeyes throughout the country.

Average Height:	Lifespan:	Year Adopted:	Scientific Name:
50 – 82 feet (15.24 – 24.99 meters)	50 years	1953	Aesculus glabra

Eastern Redbud

The skinny-trunked tree with branches covered in tiny purplish pink flowers thrives in the eastern and plains states. The stunning redbud lives only about 60 years.

No Drug Store Needed

American Indians in Oklahoma boiled the bark from this tree to make tea used to treat whooping cough. They also used the roots and inner bark from the Eastern redbud to aid those suffering from fever and nasal congestion.

Average Height:	Lifespan:	Year Adopted:	Scientific Name:
20 – 30 feet (6.09 – 9.14 meters)	50 – 70 years	1937	*Cercis canadensis*

Douglas Fir

The Douglas fir cannot rival the giant redwood in overall size, but at 300 feet (91.44 meters), it can compete in height. Its lumber makes it one of the most valuable trees of the western United States.

The 'David Douglas Fir'

This tree was named after famed botanist David Douglas. Douglas was born in Scotland in 1799, but his work in western North America gained him fame. His name is linked with hundreds of plants, mountains, rivers, and even schools. He died in Hawaii in 1834.

Average Height:	Lifespan:	Year Adopted:	Scientific Name:
195 – 245 feet (59.44 – 74.68 meters)	500 – 1,000	1939	*Pseudotsuga menziesii*

Pennsylvania

Eastern Hemlock

A visit to Ricketts Glen State Park allows one to cast eyes upon this shade-loving green tree. The eastern hemlock thrives in dark coves and gorges. It features short, soft, flat needles.

(Pennsylvania continued)

Lots of Lumber

The eastern hemlock reached the peak of its production in the 1890s. That is when Pennsylvania forests yielded more than a billion feet of hemlock lumber each year. The wood was used for a variety of construction projects. But its bark also extracted acid used to make hides for harnesses, saddles, belts, and shoes.

Average Height:	Lifespan:	Year Adopted:	Scientific Name:
70 feet (21.34 meters)	300 – 800 years	1931	*Tsoga canadensis*

 # Rhode Island

Red Maple

This fast-growing tree is often planted to beautify public parks. Its soft wood makes cheap furniture. The tree also produces sugar, but not nearly as much as the sugar maple.

The Perfect Tree for Red Lovers

People who like the color red can enjoy this tree all year. It features red in each of the four seasons. There are red buds in the winter, flowers in the spring, leaf stalks in the summer, and foliage in the fall. That brilliant color, as well as a tolerance to a variety of soils, make the red maple a popular planting tree.

Average Height:	Lifespan:	Year Adopted:	Scientific Name:
60 – 90 feet (18.29 – 27.43 meters)	80 – 100 years	1964	*Acer rubrum*

South Carolina

Sabal Palmetto

South Carolina adopted this tree to honor its place in history. A fort built from palmetto logs absorbed the impact of cannon balls fired by the British during the Revolutionary War.

Embracing a Tree

The palmetto was added to the state flag in 1860. That was the year South Carolina broke free from the United States and joined the Confederacy. The Civil War began a year later. It had many years earlier adopted the Palmetto State nickname.

Average Height:	Lifespan:	Year Adopted:	Scientific Name:
40 – 50 feet (12.19 – 15.24 meters)	200 – 300 years	1939	*Sabal palmetto*

South Dakota

Black Hills Spruce

The only spruce native to South Dakota thrives in a few southwest counties. It is nearly identical to the white spruce. But it boasts a greater tolerance to heat and drought.

(South Dakota continued)

The Great State Debate

Many South Dakota officials opposed making the Black Hills spruce the state tree. Some believed the cottonwood was a better choice. Others thought the cedar would better represent the state. But the Black Hills spruce was finally accepted.

Average Height:	Lifespan:	Year Adopted:	Scientific Name:
40 – 60 feet (12.19 –18.29 meters)	150 – 350 years	1947	*Picea glauca*

★ ★ ★ ★ ★ ★ ★ ★ ★ Tennessee ★ ★ ★ ★ ★ ★ ★ ★ ★

Tulip Poplar

This was chosen as the state tree because pioneers used it to build houses, barns, and canoes. Its name is misleading. It is actually part of the magnolia family.

The Fiddle Tree

Why is the tulip poplar sometimes known as the fiddle tree? Because the oddly shaped leaves that grow from its branches resemble small violins. And that musical instrument is also known as a fiddle.

Average Height:	Lifespan:	Year Adopted:	Scientific Name:
70 – 90 feet (21.34 – 27.43 meters)	100 – 300 years	1947	*Liriodendron tulipifera*

Pecan

Pecan pies enjoyed on Thanksgiving often feature pecans grown in Texas. The state is the largest pecan producer in America. Former governor James Hogg even requested that a Texas pecan tree be planted near his grave!

The Importance of Pecans

Pecans served as a vital food for American Indians centuries ago. They gathered and ate them with fruit, as well as vegetables such as beans and corn. They used ground pecan meal to thicken stew. They also consumed roasted pecans on long journeys when food was scarce.

Average Height:	Lifespan:	Year Adopted:	Scientific Name:
70 – 100 feet (21.34 – 30.48 meters)	40 years	1919	*Carya illinoensis*

Quaking Aspen

The quaking aspen replaced the blue spruce as the state tree in 2014. Governor Gary Herbert signed the bill making it official using pens and a desk made from the quaking aspen. The tall aspen features a thin, white bark.

A Tree for Smelly Humans!

Quaking aspen branches were once boiled down to create a cleanser. It was used to clean guns, traps, and even smelly people. Wood from this tree was also exported to make chopsticks. The strength that keeps it from splintering allows it to be made into playground equipment as well.

Average Height:	Lifespan:	Year Adopted:	Scientific Name:
20 – 80 feet (6.09 – 24.38 meters)	70 – 100 years	2014	*Picea pungens*

Sugar Maple

The largest maple syrup producer in the country is the only state to officially adopt a state flavor. What is it? Maple, of course! But folks must wait at least 22 years for sugar maples to mature.

From Sap to Syrup

Many people in Vermont are familiar with the process of turning sap into pure maple syrup. The first step is tapping into a sugar maple and collecting the sap into a bucket. It is transferred into a larger container, then taken to a sugarhouse. That is where water is boiled out of the sap over a hot fire. Festivals mark the beginning and end of the sugaring season in Vermont.

Average Height:	Lifespan:	Year Adopted:	Scientific Name:
30 – 35 feet (9.14 – 10.67 meters)	300 years	1949	*Acer saccharum*

Flowering Dogwood

American founding father Thomas Jefferson grew the flowering dogwood on his estate. It is no wonder Virginia adopted it. Its beautiful spring flowers turn white, pink, or red in full bloom.

Tall Tale or Truth?

Some people think that mange, a skin disease that affects dogs, led to the naming of this tree. The animals were cured when cleaned in a wash produced by boiling dogwood bark. But this myth has been debunked.

Average Height:	Lifespan:	Year Adopted:	Scientific Name:
20 – 30 feet (6.09 – 9.14 meters)	80 years	1956	*Cornus florida*

Western Hemlock

An Oregon newspaper teased Washington in 1946 for not having a state tree. It suggested the bushy, green western hemlock. Washington chose the red cedar instead. But it soon took the advice of its southern neighbor.

Gather Around – There's Enough Food for Everyone!

It takes 20 to 40 years for western hemlock pinecones to produce seeds. The birds then eat them along with the needles. Meanwhile, critters such as rabbits, deer, and squirrels feed off the twigs. Porcupines prefer the bark.

Average Height:	Lifespan:	Year Adopted:	Scientific Name:
164 – 213 feet (49.99 – 69.92 meters)	400 – 500 years	1947	*Tsuga heterophylla*

Sugar Maple

A 1949 vote of students and civic groups led West Virginia to adopt the sugar maple as its state tree. Yet the state is not among the top 10 maple syrup producers in the country.

The Big Tree of Bethany

Super maples can be found in all 55 counties of West Virginia. But the biggest of all sits in the Brooke County town of Bethany near the Ohio border. The 110-foot (35.53 meter) tree was once considered the largest living sugar maple in the world.

Average Height:	Lifespan:	Year Adopted:	Scientific Name:
30 – 35 feet (9.14 –10.67 meters)	300 years	1949	*Acer saccharum*

Sugar Maple

The sugar maple beat out the oak, pine, and elm in an 1893 school children's vote for state tree. The most common state tree in America brightens Wisconsin in the fall with its brilliant colors.

A Syrup Statistic

A 2014 study showed that Wisconsin ranks fourth among all states in maple syrup production. About six percent of all maple syrup produced in the United States comes from Wisconsin. Vermont is easily the leader at 42 percent, followed by New York and Maine.

Average Height:	Lifespan:	Year Adopted:	Scientific Name:
30 – 35 feet (9.14 – 10.67 meters)	300 years	1949	*Acer saccharum*

Cottonwood

This tall, skinny tree grows and dies quickly. But it provides beauty in the fall. That is when its leaves turn a bright yellow-green. The tree is named for the cottony mass of hairs around its seeds.

American Indians and the Cottonwood

Dakota Indians ate the sweet inner bark of young cottonwood trees in the spring. They also fed its branches to their horses. Another tribe that utilized the cottonwood was the Omaha. They held a sacred pole made of cottonwood while performing ceremonial dances.

Average Height:	Lifespan:	Year Adopted:	Scientific Name:
65 –130 feet (19.81 – 39.62 meters)	70 –100 years	1947	*Populus sargentii*

 # Index

www.rourkeeducationalmedia.com

PHOTO CREDITS: Cover main photo © Copyright: <a href='http://www.123rf.com/profile_vhamrick'>vhamrick / 123RF Stock Photo</a>
Small photos from Shutterstock: delaware leaf © Molotok289, New Hampshire leaf © azure1, Ohio leaf © Madlen, Rhode Island leaf © Melinda Fawver
Inside book: Alabama and North Carolina inset photo © Nikolay Kurzenko; Alaska Tree closeup © Jean Faucett; Arizona Tree © You Touch Pix of EuToch, leaf © Gill Couto; California Sequoia © Chene Taljaard, redwood © 4kclips; Blue Spruce leaf © sdrug07; Delaware leaf © Bonnie Taylor Barry; Georgia Leaf; Idaho Leaf © Marie C Fields; Illinois Tree © Malachi Jacobs; Iowa Tree © Rawin Cheasagul; Iowa Leaf © kacege; Kansas & Nebraska Tree © Steve Shoup; Kentucky Leaf © maksimee, Kentucky Tree © Peter Turner Photography; Louisiana Tree © EdwinM, leaf © jaroslava V; Maine and Michigan leaf and Tennessee tree © Peter Turner Photography; Minnesota leaf © Craig Hinton; Mississippi leaf © Pymouss44; Missouri tree © shippee, Missouri leaf © Elena Shelton; Montana tree © Bryan Chernick; New Hampshire leaves © islavicek, tree © Todd Boland ; New York leaf, Vermont, West Virginia and Wisconsin leaf © Nunun; Ohio leaves © PAKULA PIOTR; Oklahoma tree © Gau Meo, Oklahoma leaf © Yulia Kupeli; Oregon leaf © srekap, Oregon tree © Hugh K Telleria; Pennsylvania leaves © Andrew Williams; South Dakota leaf © Stephen Viszlai; Tennessee leaf © maksimee; Utah tree © Chris002; Utah leave © photowind; Virginia leaf © riphoto3, Virginia tree © GeorgeColePhoto; Washington leaf © valentyne makepie, Wyoming tree and leaves © Andrew Sabai. All images from Shutterstock.com except: Alabama and North Carolina Trees © Daniel Oines https://creativecommons.org/licenses/by/2.0/deed.en ; Alaska Tree © Graaf van Vlaanderen https://creativecommons.org/licenses/by-sa/4.0/deed.en ; Arkansas pine cone © Wasp32 https://creativecommons.org/licenses/by/4.0/deed.en ; Connecticut tree © Msact at English Wikipedia https://creativecommons.org/licenses/by-sa/3.0/deed.en; Delaware © Famartin https://creativecommons.org/licenses/by-sa/4.0/deed.en ; Georgia Tree © Ebyabe https://creativecommons.org/licenses/by-sa/3.0/deed.en; Hawaii Tree and Leaf © Forest & Kim Starr https://creativecommons.org/licenses/by/3.0/deed.en; Idaho Tree © Dcrjsr https://creativecommons.org/licenses/by/3.0/deed.en, Illinois Leaf, and Indiana Flower © Dcrjsr; Indiana Tree © Jean-Pol GRANDMONT https://creativecommons.org/licenses/by/3.0/deed.en ; Kansas & Nebraska Leaf © Laurent Bélanger https://creativecommons.org/licenses/by-sa/4.0/deed.en ; Maine and Michigan Tree courtesy of US FWS; Maryland Tree © Copyright: <a href='http://www.123rf.com/profile_vhamrick'>vhamrick / 123RF Stock Photo</a> ; Massachusetts leaf © Matt Lavin from Bozeman, Montana, USA https://creativecommons.org/licenses/by-sa/2.0/deed.en , Massachusetts Tree © Henryhartley on en.wikipedia https://creativecommons.org/licenses/by-sa/3.0/deed.en ; Minnesota Tree courtesy of US FS photo; Mississippi Tree © Pymouss44 https://creativecommons.org/licenses/by-sa/3.0/deed.en ; Montana leaf © Gerry from Fort St. John, BC, Canada https://creativecommons.org/licenses/by-sa/2.0/deed.en ; Nevada Single leaf pinyon © Dcrjsr https://creativecommons.org/licenses/by-sa/3.0/deed.en , bristlecone © Joe Decruyenaere https://creativecommons.org/licenses/by-sa/2.0/deed.en ; New Jersey leaf and New Mexico tree, New York tree, and Rhode Island tree and Rhode Island leaf close-up, and Vermont, West Virginia and Wisconsin tree © Famartin https://creativecommons.org/licenses/by-sa/4.0/deed.en ; New Mexico leaf © snowpeak https://creativecommons.org/licenses/by/2.0/deed.en ; North Dakota tree © Henryhartley on en.wikipedia https://creativecommons.org/licenses/by-sa/3.0/deed.en ; Dakota leaves © Matt Lavin from Bozeman, Montana https://creativecommons.org/licenses/by-sa/2.0/deed.en; Ohio tree courtesy of USDA; Pennsylvania tree and Texas tree © Bruce Marlin https://creativecommons.org/licenses/by-sa/3.0/deed.en ; South Dakota tree © dmcdevit https://creativecommons.org/licenses/by-sa/2.0/deed.en ; Texas leaves © The Bugwood Network at the University of Georgia and the USDA Forest Service https://creativecommons.org/licenses/by/3.0/us/deed.en; Washington tree © MPF https://creativecommons.org/licenses/by/3.0/us/deed.en;

Edited by: Keli Sipperley   Cover and Interior design by: Nicola Stratford   www.nicolastratford.com

Library of Congress PCN Data

TREES / Martin Gitlin
(STATE GUIDES)
  ISBN 978-1-68342-399-7 (hard cover)
  ISBN 978-1-68342-469-7 (soft cover)
  ISBN 978-1-68342-565-6 (e-Book)
Library of Congress Control Number: 2017931404

Rourke Educational Media
Printed in the United States of America, North Mankato, Minnesota